REALLY
HORRIBLE
JOKES

REALLY HORRIBLE ANIMAL JOKES

KAREN KING

WINDMILL BOOKS
New York

Published in 2014 by Windmill Books, An Imprint of Rosen Publishing
29 East 21st Street, New York, NY 10010

First Edition

Editors: Patience Coster and Joe Harris
US Editor: Joshua Shadowens
All Images: Shutterstock
Layout Designer: Elaine Wilkinson
Cover Designers: Elaine Wilkinson and Trudi Webb

Library of Congress Cataloging-in-Publication Data

Really horrible animal jokes / by Karen King.
    pages cm. — (Really horrible jokes)
  Includes index.
  ISBN 978-1-4777-9074-8 — ISBN 978-1-4777-9075-5 (pbk.) —
  ISBN 978-1-4777-9076-2
  1. Animals—Juvenile humor. I. Title.
  PN6231.A5K56 2014
  818'.602—dc23
                        2013021312

Printed in the USA
SL003840US

CPSIA Compliance Information: Batch #BW14WM: For Further Information contact Windmill Books, New York, New York at 1-866-478-0556

CONTENTS

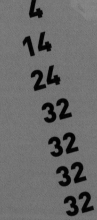

WEIRD AND WILD JOKES

What did the skunk say when the wind changed?
It's all coming back to me now.

How many skunks does it take to make a big stink?
A phew!

Why aren't elephants allowed on the beach?
Their trunks might fall down.

What's the difference between a *T. rex* and a dead skunk?
One's extinct, and the other's an ex-stinker!

There was a lady from Niger
Who went for a ride on a tiger.
Not long after that,
The tiger got fat
With the lady from Niger
inside her.

What is an elephant's favorite sport? Squash!

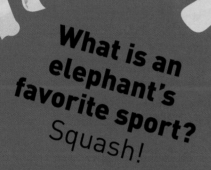

Why do ostriches have such long legs? So they can't smell their feet.

Why do gorillas have big nostrils? Have you seen the size of their fingers?!

What do you call a man who keeps a wild ferret down his pants?
Stupid!

What is a polygon?
A dead parrot.

What's wet, smelly, and goes ba-bump, ba-bump?
A skunk in a tumble dryer.

What's brown and dangerous and lives in a tree?
A coconut with a machine gun.

Why are skunks always arguing?
Because they like to raise a stink.

What do you call a bloodsucking pig?
A hampire.

What do you call a flying skunk?
A smellicopter.

What do you get if you cross an elephant with a ton of prunes?
Out of the way.

How many arms does an alligator have?
It depends on how much of its dinner it's eaten!

Why did the porcupine cross the road?
To show that he had guts.

What do you give a sick bird?
Tweetment.

Harry: Have you ever hunted bear?
James: No, but I've been on safari in my shorts.

Mary had a little bear,
To which she was quite kind.
So everywhere that Mary went,
She had a bear behind.

What do you find in an elephant graveyard?
Elephantoms.

Why did the lion eat the tightrope walker?
He wanted a well-balanced meal.

What's the difference between a coyote and a flea?
One howls on the prairie, and the other prowls on the hairy.

What do you call an exploding monkey?
A baboom!

Did you hear about the frog who had his legs chopped off?
He was very un-hoppy.

What did the lion say when he saw the kid on a skateboard?
"Meals on wheels!"

First lion: Every time I eat a priest, I feel sick.
Second lion: I know, it's hard to keep a good man down.

Hickory, dickory, dock,
Two mice ran up the clock.
The clock struck one,
But the other managed
to get away.

Why was the young kangaroo thrown out by his mother?
For jumping on the bed.

What do you call a thieving sheep?
A ram raider.

What did they call the canary that flew into the pastry dish?
Tweetie Pie.

What do you get if you cross an elephant with a kangaroo?
Holes all over Australia.

Knock, knock!
Who's there?
Panther.
Panther who?
Panther what you wear on your legth.

How do you stop a fish from smelling?
Cut off its nose.

What do you call a large African mammal with a runny nose?
A rhi-snot-erous.

How do porcupines play leapfrog?
Very carefully.

What's green and gross and lives under the sea?
Shark snot!

What eats all
the animals two
by two?
Noah's shark!

What's green, slimy,
and six feet long?
An elephant's
booger!

Knock, knock!
Who's there?
Lionel.
Lionel who?
Lionel roar if you
step on its tail.

Waiter! Bring me a
crocodile sandwich
immediately!
I'll make it snappy, sir!

There was a young lady from Crewe,
Who found a dead mouse in her stew.
Said the waiter: "Don't shout and wave it about,
Or the others will all want one, too!"

What do sharks call human children?
Hors d'oeuvres.

What did the jungle explorer say to the leech?
So long, sucker!

What do sharks play fetch with?
Fish sticks.

What's green, has four legs, and a tail?
A seasick rat.

What do you get if you cross a bear with a cow pie?
Winnie the Pooh.

What did the evil chicken lay?
Deviled eggs.

What did the hen say when her eggs hatched?
Chick it out!

Why did the dirty chicken cross the road?
For some fowl purpose!

What's black and white and green and brown?
A cow with a runny nose in a muddy field.

Waiter, waiter! This chicken is covered in spots.
Don't worry, sir, it's only chicken pox.

14

Mary had a little lamb,
It ran around the shops.
Then it crossed the road one day
And ended up as chops.

What's invisible and smells like carrots?
Rabbit farts.

What do you call a man in a bathtub full of cow pies?
An in-cowpoop!

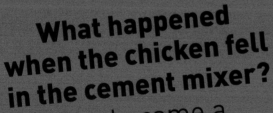

What happened when the chicken fell in the cement mixer?
She became a bricklayer.

What has fangs and webbed feet?
Count Duckula.

Did you hear about the cow that forgot how to make milk?
It was an udder catastrophe.

What goes Ooooo! Oooooo!
A cow with no lips!

Where do you find a chicken with no legs?
Exactly where you left it.

What do you get if you sit under a cow?
A pie in the face!

What do you get if you cross King Kong with a parakeet?
A messy cage.

Mary had a little lamb,
It rolled around in poo.
And everywhere that Mary went,
Her smelly lamb went, too.

Why did half a chicken cross the road?
To get to her other side.

What do you call a sheep with a machine gun?
Lambo.

Don't ever kiss your bunny,
When its nose is runny.
The snot will taste all funny,
And stick to you like honey!

A hungry little wolf cub,
Looking for his pack,
Came upon a duckling,
And ate it as a snack.
And now instead of howling,
The cub keeps going quack!

Why do mice need oiling?
Because they squeak.

Why is a turkey like an evil little creature?
Because it's always a-goblin.

What do you call a cow with no legs?
Ground beef.

What do you get from nervous cows?
Milkshakes.

How do you know if your cat's eaten a duckling?
It looks down in the mouth.

Which song does a cat like best?
Three Blind Mice.

What has four legs, whiskers, a tail, and flies?
A dead cat.

What type of horses only go out at night?
Nightmares.

How do you know that owls are smarter than chickens?
Have you ever heard of Kentucky Fried Owl?

Knock, knock!
Who's there?
Goose.
Goose who?
Goose who's knocking at your door!

What did the black cat do when its tail was cut off?
It went to a re-tail store.

What's worse than a bull in a china shop?
A porcupine in a balloon factory.

Two cows were talking in the field.
Cow 1: Are you worried about this mad cow disease?
Cow 2: Why should I be? I'm a penguin.

When is it unlucky to see a black cat?
When you are a mouse.

Little sausage dog,
Walks across the street.
Here comes a speeding car,
Now it's sausage meat!

My dog saw a sign saying "Wet Paint."
So he did!

What do you get if you cross a cat with a canary?
A full tummy.

What do cats like for breakfast?
Mice Krispies.

There once was a large tabby cat,
Who swallowed a whole baseball bat.
He swallowed the ball,
The bases and all,
So the baseball team clobbered him flat.

What kind of market do dogs avoid?
Flea markets.

Tim: This loaf of bread is nice and warm.
Sarah: It should be, the cat's been sitting on it all day!

What's the difference between a maggot and a cockroach?
Cockroaches crunch more when you eat them.

Which animals didn't go to the ark in pairs?
Maggots. They went in apples!

How do you keep flies out of the kitchen?
Put a bucket of manure in the hallway.

Why didn't the viper viper nose?
Because the adder adder 'ankie.

Why did the flea flee?
Because the spider spied 'er!

What do worms leave around the top of bathtubs?
The scum of the earth.

What did one maggot say to the other maggot?
What's a nice girl like you doing in a joint like this?

What do you get if you cross a bee with a skunk?
A creature that stinks and stings.

What's the maggot army called?
The apple corps.

What goes red, green, red, green?
A frog in a blender.

What lies on the ground, 100 feet in the air, and smells?
A dead centipede.

How do frogs die?
They Kermit suicide.

What do you call a worm that won't sit still?
A squirm!

What did the slug say when it was thrown over the fence?
How slime flies!

What happened when a daddy longlegs crawled into the salad?
It became a daddy shortlegs.

What's the definition of a nervous breakdown?
A chameleon on a tartan rug.

What sort of fish can't swim?
A dead one.

What's green and dangerous?
A frog with a hand grenade.

What happens if you eat a frog?
You'll croak in no time.

Waiter, waiter! There's a maggot in my soup.
Don't worry, sir, it won't live long in that stuff!

What's white on the outside and green in the middle?
A frog sandwich.

What are the most faithful insects on the planet?
Fleas. Once they find someone they like, they'll never leave them.

What did the fisherman use as a bookmark?
A flatfish to mark his plaice.

Knock, knock!
Who's there?
Woodworm.
Woodworm who?
Woodworm cake be enough, or would you like two?

What's the difference between school lunches and a pile of slugs?
School lunches come on a plate.

Knock Knock!
Who's there?
Thumping.
Thumping who?
Thumping green and slimy is climbing up your back!

Little Miss Muffet
sat on a tuffet,
Eating a bowl of stew.
Along came a spider,
And sat down beside her,
So she ate that up, too.

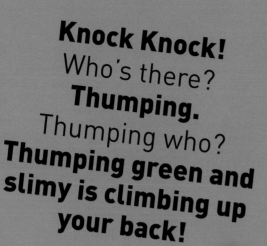

Waiter, waiter! What's wrong with this fish?
Long time no sea, sir!

What do you call a snake that builds houses?
A boa constructor!

What's worse than finding a worm in your apple?
Finding half a worm in your apple!

Knock, knock!
Who's there?
Moth.
Moth who?
Moth get myself a key.

What's yellow, wriggly, and dangerous?
A maggot with attitude.

Which hand would you grab a poisonous snake with?
Somebody else's!

What did the butterfly say to the cockroach?
Quit bugging me!

What kind of fish do Eskimos catch?
Ice skates!

What's the difference between a worm and an apple?
Have you tried eating worm pie?

What's wet and slippery and likes Latin American music?
A conga eel.

What do you get when you cross a flea with a rabbit?
Bugs Bunny.

What's green and slimy and found at the North Pole?
A lost frog.

Glossary

corps (KOR) A section of the army.

deviled eggs (DEH-vild EGZ) Hard-boiled eggs filled with a mixture of yolk, mustard, and mayonnaise.

flea market (FLEE MAR-kut) An outdoor market that sells second-hand goods.

grenade (gruh-NAYD) A small bomb that is thrown by hand.

Latin America (LAH-tin ah-MEH-rih-kuh) The areas of the American continent where the main national language is Spanish or Portugese.

Niger (NYE-jur) A country in West Africa.

phantom (FAN-tum) A ghost.

polygon (PAH-lee-gon) A shape with straight sides, such as a square or triangle.

Further Reading

Connolly, Sean. *The Animal Antics Joke Book*. Laugh Out Loud. New York: Windmill Books, 2014.

Hawkins, Jay. *Really Horrible Animal Facts*. Really Horrible Facts. New York: Windmill Books, 2014.

Weintraub, Aileen. *The Everything Kids' Gross Jokes Book*. Avon, MA: Adams Media, 2005.

Websites

For web resources related to the subject of this book, go to: www.windmillbooks.com/weblinks and select this book's title.

Index